Where X Marks the Spot

OTHER BOOKS BY BILL ZAVATSKY

POETRY
Theories of Rain and Other Poems
For Steve Royal and Other Poems

TRANSLATION
The Poems of A. O. Barnabooth by Valery Larbaud
with Ron Padgett
Earthlight: Poems by André Breton
with Zack Rogow

EDUCATION
The Whole Word Catalog 2
co-edited with Ron Padgett

WHERE X MARKS THE SPOT

Bill Zavatsky

Hanging Loose Press
Brooklyn, New York

Published by Hanging Loose Press, 231 Wyckoff Street, Brooklyn, NY 11217-2208. All rights reserved. No part of this book may be reproduced without the publisher's written permission, except for brief quotations in reviews.

Hanging Loose Press thanks the New York State Council on the Arts for its generous support of the publication of this book.

www.hangingloosepress.com

Printed in the United States of America
10 9 8 7 6 5 4 3 2 1

Cover art, *Where X Marks the Spot*, by the author. Mixed media, 9" x 12", 2004.
Cover design by Marie Carter
Author photo by Margaretta K. Mitchell © 1997

Some of these poems, often in earlier versions, appeared in the following magazines and anthologies, to whose editors and publishers the author would like to express his gratitude:
Red M, Marxist Perspectives, Poetry Society of America Newsletter, The Teachers and Writers Newsletter, Joe Soap's Canoe, Cover, "Metropolitan Diary" of the New York *Times, Hanging Loose, Columbia Review, Skanky Possum, SUN, Poets: On the Line, Pemmican* (online), *The Poetry Project Newsletter, PoetryMagazine.com.*

The Face of the Poet, a portfolio of portraits by Alex Katz; *Baseball I Gave You All the Best Years of My Life,* edited by Kevin Kerrane and Richard Grossinger; *Diamonds Are Forever: Poets and Writers on Baseball,* edited by Peter H. Gordon, with Sydney Waller and Paul Weinman; *Coming of Age Volume Two: Literature About Youth and Adolescence* and in *Sports in Literature,* Second Edition, both edited by Bruce Emra; *Out of This World: The Poetry Project at the St. Mark's Church-in-the-Bowery, An Anthology 1966-1991,* edited by Anne Waldman; "Elegy" appeared on the sleeve of the Warner Bros. LP and Warner/Rhino CD *You Must Believe in Spring* by Bill Evans; *Reading Jazz* edited by David Meltzer; *The Jazz Poetry Anthology,* edited by Sascha Feinstein and Yusef Komunyakaa; *Educating the Imagination Volumes One and Two: Essays & Ideas for Teachers & Writers,* edited by Christopher Edgar and Ron Padgett; *Up Late: American Poetry Since 1970,* selected and introduced by Andrei Codrescu; *The Face of Poetry,* edited by Zack Rogow and Margaretta K. Mitchell; *Will Work for Peace: New Political Poems,* edited by Brett Axel; *Present/Tense: Poets in the World,* edited by Mark Pawlak.

Several of these poems also appeared in a chapbook published *hors commerce* called *For Steve Royal and Other Poems.*

Library of Congress Cataloging-in-Publication Data available on request.

ISBN: 1-931236-67-4 (paper)
ISBN: 1-931236-68-2 (cloth)

 Produced at The Print Center, Inc. 225 Varick St., New York, NY 10014, a non-profit facility for literary and arts-related publications. (212) 206-8465

CONTENTS

met Pablo Neruda

For Harvey Shapiro

Poet, mentor, friend

And thoughtfully Telémakhos replied:

"Friend, let me put it in the plainest way.
My mother says I am his son; I know not
surely. Who has known his own engendering?
I wish at least I had some happy man
as father, growing old in his own house—
but unknown death and silence are the fate
of him that, since you ask, they call my father."

Odyssey, I
Translated by Robert Fitzgerald

Where X Marks the Spot

104 BUS UPTOWN

How bad can it be,
dear wacky New York City,
when the first twelve lines
of *The Love Song of J. Alfred Prufrock*
blink down at me
from a poster on this bus
brought to us
courtesy of the MTA
and the Poetry Society of America
(of which, incredibly, I am a member!)
and, to its right, above the rear door,
another poster: Charles Reznikoff's little poem
about how "the lights go out—"
in the subway
"but are on again in a moment,"
a poem I will be teaching to my students
in a few weeks' time.
And perched in the center back seat
(she got on at Seventh Avenue and 42nd Street),
sitting all alone, as if on a little stage
lit by the bus-window daylight of midtown New York,
the beautiful actress Beverly D'Angelo
whom I can't bring myself to ask
if she *is* Beverly D'Angelo, except that I
recognize the perfection of her charming overbite
as she chews gum like mad over wild blue eyes agog,
behaving as if she's never sat on a bus before
or as if she expects a passenger to leap up
at any moment and cry, "Action!,"
with the cameras rolling like the eyes in my head
as I turn now and again to look at her
in her white jacket and skirt that don't
quite match, a silk turquoise blouse
that color-keys her enormous eyes

(which just got off with the rest of her
at 57th and Eighth), and I'm lucky
enough to have been handed this
piece of paper twenty minutes ago
by someone on the street who must be
a secret agent for poetry, though it seems
to be merely an advertisement flyer
for 45th Street Photo, on the back of which
I've just written this poem

Woman Walking

toward me, holding
in her outstretched arms
the plastic bag with her
cleaning in it that looks
like the dead Jesus cradled
in her arms, her face the
Mother Mary face of sorrow itself
the kind of Irish face
I went to school with, the face
that taught me about grief—
and so she passes me by

EVITA

In the middle of a nearly empty subway car
sits a lovely young black woman
whose face has been painted completely white.
Exaggerated lashes, like flower petals,
spring from her eyes in blue paint.
Otherwise, she wears carpenter jeans
and a red leotard top. Nonchalantly she stares
at the ceiling, arms folded demurely,
as if this were how she always traveled.
At the far end of the car, in a heavy Spanish accent,
a man begins to sing loudly: "E-viiiiiii-*ta!*
E-viiiiiii-*ta!*
You were sup-posed to, Be im-mor-tal,
That's all you asked for, Not much to ask for!
E-viiiiiii-*ta!* E-viiiiiii-*ta!*"
He rocks back and forth to the rhythm of the train,
singing his heart out, then suddenly
catches sight of the mime-faced woman.
With a wave of his hands, he jerks his body backwards
in a perfect silent-movie double take.
He freezes, mouth popped open, staring at her.
Then, muttering something in Spanish—his secret name
for the woman, his own Evita conjured by his singing—
he kicks into a wild flamenco dance,
banging his heels, clapping his hands
above his head like castanets as he whirls,
mouthing words lost in the train's roar.
Dazed, he circles the car pole
in the ecstasy of his trance, too absorbed to notice
that the woman left the train at 50th Street.
Halfway to the next station, still oblivious
of her departure, or mourning it,
he clutches the pole and begins to sing again.
"E-viiiiiii-*ta!*

Not much to ask for, That's all you wanted!"
At Columbus Circle the doors open.
A bespectacled young woman with a violin case
steps into the doorway. For a moment she hesitates,
turning to say a few words of goodbye to a young man.
Immobilized, our singer stands behind her, face
churning with new emotion, body slowly rising
to full height. "Hey!" he screams at her, gesticulating.
"Hey! C'mon—in or out, in or out!" Flapping his hands,
"I gotta get to work!" he hollers. Terrified,
the woman jumps back onto the platform,
into the arms of her friend
as the train doors bang together.
"E-viiiiiii-*ta!*" the singer cries
as the train crashes forward, "E-viiiiiii-*ta!*
You were sup-posed to, Be im-mor-tal!
E-viiiiiii-*ta!*"

CHANTILLY

to Serge Fauchereau

Those fish down
there, those carp
nosing the surface
into little waves,
snouts like piglets',
those fish are
the carp Apollinaire
wrote about. "And
they live so long!"
my French friend said,
who took me to Chantilly
castle to see them
floating lazily
through reflections
of our faces, clouds,
the blue sky drifting
like water beneath
the stone bridges, floated
into Apollinaire's
eye, these same
carp, babies then,
and poor Guillaume
alive as me then, too,
young, smiling that big
fat smile of a happy fish,
alive for a few moments
with the secret
of living in the 20th century

On the Rainbow

Once the rainbow meant something—
A promise after the storm.
Now I see its emblem sewn
to the jackets of street kids
drifting, smashed on the latest drug,
who must be looking for that something
as they stagger towards Times Square.

Black Elk, Lakota seer, painted a rainbow
on his tepee to remind him that its arches
marked the entrance to the Other World.
There the Grandfathers, Powers of the Universe,
awaited him with thunder and prancing horses.
At Wounded Knee, amidst the piles of bodies,
he wept for the ruined vision of his childhood.

Keats blamed "cold philosophy"
for clipping the angel's wings;
others claim that science wrecked the rainbow.
I don't know how, but it happens.
Yesterday we met a bright young student
and later, speaking of him, my wife remarked:
"How wonderful to be young, to have
that eagerness for everything!"
She is forty; I am forty-one.

I still believe in the rainbow.
I wore a pretty button with a rainbow
in the '60s, when everyone wore buttons.
Probably I have it tucked away somewhere.
I even remember what the button meant:
the "Rainbow Coalition" that saw hope
in the coming together of people of every race
—all the colors of the human spectrum—

and how the decade ended in strife and division
between those who might have joined hands.

London, summer of 1971, I caught on film
a rainbow overarching the whole city.
Years later, sitting in an outdoor café,
my French friend Serge and I looked up to see
a rainbow circling the Empire State Building,
flowing bannerlike across the skyline.
At that moment he jumped up, crying, "Bill!"
then ran away, leaving me nonplussed.
I thought he had cried *my* name,
transfixed by some revelation of the rainbow.

But it was another Bill, a poet whom by chance
I was writing or had just written about
and didn't want to meet. And so I sat, sipping
my beer, studying the sky, as did others
sitting or strolling. Maybe the point is
that no one knows when a rainbow is coming
or what it may leave in its wake,
"wake" as in death, the end of aspiration
or as in "Wake up!"—Wordsworth's cry:
> *My heart leaps up when I behold*
> *A rainbow in the sky!*

Which shows that when a poem is heading
nowhere, one tactic is to borrow stripes
from a poet of higher rank and stitch them on.
Maybe that's what the kids feel,
stumbling out of the Port Authority Terminal,
bright rainbow insignia over their hearts,
eating their street dinner, staring at the lights

New Year's Eve 1989

Up on the roof, waiting for the fireworks to begin
in warm winter rain, a moment ago I stepped
from the elevator into the black air
of an almost New Year
and need a minute to catch my breath
at the spread of city open to my eye.
I can't go to the edge; I never could.
The old fear of height still troubles me,
the sensation that nothing can be under me
if I am surrounded by mist and rain
and all of the dark night air we breathe.
Even a glimpse at the treetops in the park,
with its slick crisscrossing roads that plunge
into the jumbled panorama of East Side Manhattan,
hysterical tonight with its own incandescence,
gives me the willies. I feel as if
I were standing on the deck of a showboat of a cloud
as it drifts down some dark river, waiting for it
to bang into some other building's fifteenth floor.
How can these old people hunch the railing,
hoisting their plastic glasses of champagne
from under dripping umbrellas, as if
they drank the rain as they laugh
their analyses of the weather?
Maybe now, like me, they have nothing to lose.
I moved in three weeks ago; this is my first trip
to the roof. I don't want to die tonight,
the first fatality of 1990! There's too much of me
I left in pieces last year, oh, the whole last decade!
But I'm up here to distract myself, temporarily,
from what I don't want or can't have
in the way of love. . . . That must be
the Triborough Bridge, tied in its strings
of blue lights, and I can see in Central Park

the skating rink, like a scoured mirror below,
where some madman waves a red lantern; he
must be drunk. I have only sipped a speck of Drambuie,
which I didn't carry in my Coca-Cola glass
up to these festivities. This is the first New Year's
I've spent alone in twenty, twenty-two years.
I never could go to the edge; but I did.
Out there in the dark: my marriage, the woman
I loved badly, as she did me, or none too well;
the places we lived; the apartment I once half-owned;
the thousands of books I had to leave behind
(though I am to be granted library privileges)
and the black and white cat I really miss.
My wife's with her friends tonight somewhere in Brooklyn;
friends of mine out there, too, though I don't know
where. It's just like me to move in the middle
of a telephone company strike. Thus, no calls
from anyone—and I don't even have
a telephone yet, so who could call? Damp but trying
to smile, I eye the revelers. Two young men
and their enormous girlfriends have joined us,
really large women who carry balloons, all ready
to froth in merry champagne. We check
our watches to the screams from swarms
of apartment windows to the west
as the sky lights up with the first furious
bombardment of colored shells. I can see that
red lantern swinging toward the rockets—aha!
So it wasn't a drunk, but the fireworks engineer
preparing to blow the year's last sky
to smithereens for our delight!
I like to follow the tiny spurts of flame
from the launching pad in their heavenward trajectory
as much as I like the rockets' red glare,
the bombs bursting in air, which give proof
to the night that I am still here, hands
jammed in the pockets of my sodden raincoat,
face dripping with rain, hat soaked, wondering

if the skinny guy in the army jacket behind me
(who looks just like I did in the sixties)
is mumbling his way into a combat flashback
and ready to hurl me over the edge of the roof
and into kingdom come. I guess not yet. We've
survived the first blasts of spinning green,
corkscrews of spangled flame, buds of fireballs
spewed in arching gold sprays, the whistling fire-fish
that curl and howl as they flare, falling to ash.
Screaming its head off, the New York New Year enters.
I feel sad that beautiful things must die,
even shadows made of smoke and flame,
whatever I thought I had made out of my life—
music, poems, books, kisses, a little useless fame.
The army guy behind me grumbles at the haze
of rocket smoke that coils around the trees,
then tumbles up into the air toward Harlem.
That bump and thud and bump sound everywhere,
more clouds smacking each other head-on.
The flashes of the explosions are close enough
to touch if you wanted to burn your fingers
on the sky, and the glare rocks our shadows back
against the brick, as if chaos snapped
our pictures in the dark. I smile for my portrait,
curious at the New Year, smelling the acrid smoke
of the one we've just destroyed. Then I squeeze into
the tiny elevator car with the others, anonymous,
reconciled to be so, back to my little apartment
and the waiting glass of amber drink I'll raise,
only half in jest, to my new life.

Reading Roque Dalton, Smoking a Nicaraguan Cigar

1.
Roque, you wrote that your prison guard
"suggested that perhaps I could write him a poem . . .
so he could keep it for a souvenir
after they killed me."
                              Well, wasn't he
one of "the people" you said you wrote for?
Whose lives you said were your "ongoing concern"?
You worried about poetry, too,
in the three lines you wrote with this title:

The Art of Poetry 1974

> *Poetry*
> *Forgive me for having helped you understand*
> *that you aren't just made out of words.*

Eventually someone did kill you,
someone from a rival leftist group
in your native El Salvador.

I've lived a year longer
than you did.
I haven't smoked a cigar
in two years, but now I'm hooked again,
puffing on a Nicaraguan stogie,
55¢, the last of a bundle found
in a little tobacco shop on 38th.
"The guy who sold them
stopped coming around," the owner said.
"They blew up the factories in their revolution,"
he shrugged. What he meant was, "How stupid
can you get?"
                  "I'm glad they did, I'm glad
they had their revolution," I answered back.

"The Somozas were monsters—they bled the country dry!"
He winced. I felt ashamed
before his reddening face as he shrugged again.
"I got them on a deal," he said,
almost apologizing, wary
of offending a new customer.

2.
All I know about Roque Dalton
is what I read in *Social Text*—
a brief biography, eleven pages of poems,
and the little book of his writing
published by the Curbstone Press of Connecticut,
Poetry & Militancy in Latin America.
One source claims that "while he was in jail
under sentence of death, an earthquake
destroyed the cell walls, allowing him to escape."
Not a bad beginning for a myth, for a middle-class boy
brought up in Jesuit schools—miracle
in the service of the Revolution!
I sat in those schools myself
here in North America,
soaking up the holy stories
of the gentle Christ who fed the multitudes
with a few loaves and fishes,
the Christ they couldn't kill.
I too waited for the walls to collapse.
I wonder if the guard returned
after the earth had split open
to find that Roque had vanished,
the guard who asked for the souvenir poem,
the way the disciples returned to find
the tomb of Jesus—empty.

3.
I have never been locked in a cell,
waiting to be killed.
Smoking this Nicaraguan cigar

is the easiest thing in the world.
The "people" Dalton speaks of
so lovingly in one of his essays
are often hard for me to love.
When I'd find the splintered glass
of their bottles along my street
or hurry my wife past someone pissing
against the next-door building,
though the free toilets of the Port Authority
are clean and open a block away, I'd fly
into a rage. In the safety of my apartment,
the ugliest things within me smashed
against the bars of their cage.
I don't know where I want the whores
and their tricks to go, screaming
all night in the parking lot
below our window. I'd think of buying
a little gun, a BB gun, to shoot
and scare them away. I'd think of leading
men from our building
armed with baseball bats
into the parking lot at three a.m.
I am sick and angry to be woken
by crazed voices, monster radios,
the slamming car doors and racing engines
of people who don't live here.
Roque, you would point at me and say:
"Don't let your anger go out at the victims!
Take your baseball team over to Trump Tower
or the Museum of Modern Art, where Lissitzky
sits in the gift shop window, his genius reduced
to a matching cup and saucer!"
I know you're right, Roque, but sometimes
I don't care. I take my life in my hands
and tell the kid in the doorway:
"Do I go piss on the street where you live?"
I rant and stomp around the rooms,
frightening even myself as I carry on.

4.
Roque, you must have seen this, too,
the bum wrapped around his bottle of Night Train,
struggling to focus on the limousines
that speed to the Saturday matinee
at the Metropolitan Opera, tickets
$38.00 $45.00 $75.00
(maybe more by the time this gets published)—
government-subsidized art
that only the rich can afford.
You must have seen a bum like this
shaking his head over where they get the money
when 55¢ in change
is tough enough to scrounge.
In these hard days
even the liquor store on Ninth and 44th
has closed its doors.
The painted brick flakes away
where the winos used to drowse
out of the sun, where one guy
demanded a quarter
to hail me a cab.
I told him I worked damn hard
for what I made.
Who can dig down
in his pocket every time?
And what can poetry buy
in the world of pennies
and limousines? . . .
You can't change much
by giving your change away.
Or only for a little while,
a little sleep in the shade
of an empty storefront
as the shadows of the limousines whoosh by.

5.
My second cigar tastes as good
as the first. I wonder if Dalton
smoked cigars, these sweet Nicaraguan cigars,
and the earth-dark cigars of Cuba
where he lived for a time in exile,
as I have been in exile
from the people I seem powerless to know
or help, or sometimes even feel compassion towards
in their violence, in their sadness,
in the strangeness they must feel
as I walk their streets, smoking
my big cigar, trying to pass them by
invisibly, like this smoke from my mouth
drifting into the air.

6. *Coda*
The poem should have ended there.
That last dramatic image as the smoke
of language eddies from my cigar.
                              On a note
of liberal despair, informed by concern,
leaving in your mind the image
of a man, intelligent, sincere
if a bit naive, struggling to find
the truth.
              And what is the truth?
I am no subway vigilante. Inside me
there is love—and so much anger!
But what do I know of these faces in the street,
the ones I fear, the ones I see my face in?
The faces of color, or speaking another language,
hurrying their way to work, terrified also,
all of us faces turned down or turning away in fear.

What do I know except these confused ideas
I spout in the purity of my hopelessness,
wondering if anything can be done.

I know I can't take up the cross;
it's too slippery with blood.
Roque, what if I took up the gun
the way you did?
Once I learned to pull the trigger,
could I ever put it down?

SKELETONS

What skeletons most want
is to have their lips back
so that they can stop smiling
that horrible bony smile
of eternal dead teeth
and can kiss someone
or something once in a while,
a cheek, a key, a flower,
while they hang around
waiting for the rest
of their bodies to grow back

BALD

In the mirror it's plain to see:
soon I'll be bald, like the two faceless men
staring at each other in the word SOON.
Left profile crowding mirror, I can still pretend
it isn't happening—enough tangled skeins
of hair hide the gleam. But from the right,
where the wave lifts, I don't have to push my face
close to see it winking at me—
the mysterious island of my skull,
the dinky coastline of my baby head
swimming back to me at last.
Through the sparse shore weeds
that dot the beach (I mean my
miserable hairs), it glints. Soon
I'll crawl ashore where all uncles live—
the ones who never grew any hair,
their clown cannibal heads hilarious
in photographs, glaring like chromosomes
from dresser picture frames the way
they always did when I and my cousins
stopped short in a game of tag to stare at them,
trapped under glass in their dumb grown-up world,
a phrenology of how I'd never be. Then
two years ago I saw my head in a three-way mirror
buying a coat: three pink slivers of skin like slices
of pizza radiated from my part. The overhead lighting
shriveled my scalp, scorching my silk purse
to a sow's ass. Soon the morning hairs in the sink
reached out their arms and wailed to me.
Soon the moonlight with its chilly hands
seized my cranium, taking measurements.
Everybody kept quiet. I was the last to know.
Yes, I'm drifting closer. Closer
to the desert island where I'll live out my days

training to be ever more the skeleton
that's taking over my body pore by pore.
Hair by hair its fingerbone scissors snip me
away, I who in the sixties fell in love
with my own hair! Who swooned among
battalions of Narcissuses over the ripples
our long tresses made in that mirror
of our generation, the President's face!
I who have always known
that Death is a haircut!
Walking the streets I pause to study my scalp
where it hangs in a butcher shop window,
reflected beside the other meat.
Under my breath I sing the song I'm learning
that goes, "Bald is anonymous . . . bald is goodbye."
I will not grow the hair above my ear
until it's ten feet long, then drape it suavely
over the empty parking lot atop my head
where the forest used to loom, then plaster it down
with goo. No, I don't want a toupee
to fall in my soup, or a hair transplant
driven into my brain with giant needles!
I shoo away the mysterious weave
spun from the dead hair of unfortunate ones,
rich only in what grows from their head.
I reject the compensatory beard—I refuse
to live my life upside-down!
I prepare myself to receive the litanies
chanted by the kids as I enter the classroom:
"Chrome dome, marble head, baldy bean, skin head,
Bowling ball brain, reflector head, bubble top. . . ."
I urge them on in the making of metaphor!
I am content to merge with the reflection
of every bald barber who ever adjusted my head.
I am enchanted, so late, to be becoming
someone else—the face in the mirror which,
by the time I claim it, won't even look like me!
I am thrilled to realize that the scythe

of the grim reaper is nothing more
than a cheap plastic comb
you can buy in any drugstore,
and even its teeth fall out

SLEEP

I lean back comfortably on a couch pillow,
open my book: in seconds I'm asleep.
I had planned to read the book; I expected
to do almost anything but fall asleep.
But there I am—asleep. Just look at me!
I guess I could make myself "sit up straight."
The truth is, I don't own a decent chair
with a high back where I could rest my head,
a comfortable chair in which I could read
beneath a strong light, and . . . drift off to sleep.
I have been falling asleep my whole life,
not really wanting or expecting to. . . .
As a boy my mother let me sleep late
on Saturdays—that's where it all began!
Outside my window neighbor kids would scream
my name, my name, my name, then march away
flinging baseballs, snowballs, as over I
rolled for another forty thousand winks.
So it began, and now I find I lack
the will to reverse the slow inclination
of my head in mid-nod, neck going jelly,
the delicious honeying of the eyelids
smeared with torpor, the slackening ebb and flow
of the breathing chest and the coming dream.
Writing this, I am of course awake, or
so I think. I'm awake, but thinkers say
that one may sleep thinking one is awake.
And finally one may not be "one" at all,
but two—the one asleep and the one awake;
the one awake taking the sleeper's hand.
Thus I pace about my sleeping form and brood.
And now it seems that I recognize myself
in lighted scenes, like those upon a stage.
Over there, on that couch, I'm twenty-three;

drooping, my eyelids click shut by degrees.
Moby Dick slides from my hand. There, at thirty,
again I try to read it, but my flagging
hand slides the volume onto my chest; buoyed
by waves of breathing years, I've launched entire
libraries on my after-dinner naps.
1968: I'll read *Oblomov*.
Each time Oblomov fell asleep, I did!
Here I am on fifty morning trains, headed
to Mineola, Armonk, Sheepshead Bay;
to Springfield, Massachusetts; to Ronkonkoma.
(What the hell am I doing in Ronkonkoma?)
I'm headed nowhere! I have no head, it's
stuck in a dream, clamped in a guillotine.
The conductor's voice falls: "Mineola!
Station stop, Mineola!"—my head thumps
to the floor against my briefcase, yawns up
at me from cigarette butts, juice containers.
"This head of mine dates from the Hippie Era,"
I explain, as I rush past the conductor
onto the drizzly Mineola platform,
grizzled head of long hair tucked under arm.
The head, it blinks and smiles. Back on my neck
it scans the parked cars for the matron waiting
to whisk me to some drowsy second grade
where I shall teach the children poe-uh-tree.
But Edgar Allan Poe was not a tree,
I muse, and do I say "pome" or "po-em"?
Mispronunciation and its effects
on the younger generation. "Poem. Po-em."
It's awfully early. Really, I should be
asleep, jammed in my red pajamas, crammed
under sheet and blanket and quilt. But there's
Mrs. Norton, beeping her horn and waving.
I run through the rain, hop in the warm car,
and we're off! "Let me fill you in," she says,
"on who you'll be working with, and the kids—
are they thrilled The Poet's coming!" I stroke

my wife's warm buttocks, she presses so close,
rolling her hips against me as I smooth
my hand along her steamy belly. "Two
sugars, please, Mrs. Norton!" I nearly
scream as she slides a hot coffee container
into my cupped hands, directly on top
of my daydream. She stomps the gas to make
a light. "Can't letcha be late today!"
she tweets. How wide awake she looks, I marvel.
That there are people living on my planet
with eyes so blue and skin so freshly scrubbed,
rolling their hips against me as I smooth
my hand across—wait a second! I seem
to have drifted off again, lulled
by the whack of the tires that hit where slab
of cement joins slab of cement, *ka-chunk, ka-
chunk, ka-chunk, ka-chunk, ka-*

CLASS WALK WITH NOTEBOOKS AFTER STORM

"These puddles floating
down this street
must lead somewhere . . ."

Or so I think
but don't tell
the whole third grade

trailing behind me,
stopped to lean on cars
or telephone poles,

scrawling their seeing
on spiral pads
or blowy paper sheets.

I want them to stalk
their own lives, to see
that all of matter matters

and so—outdoors! Arms
flying into sleeves
down rickety school stairs

into the rain-wet streets
all eyes and ears
with ballpoint pens alert

to make sense of this town
that's made them much
of what they are and will be.

A wandering pooch
plots afternoon smells.
I too lead my students

by the nose, exhibiting
everything: the basketball
ogled by a fishtank fish

in Don's Hobby Store window;
the candy store's weathered wood
"like those old gravestones"

notes one melancholy boy
I can't help patting
on the head

he reminds me so
of my gloomy self
at that age, when

"Smile!" my parents chirped
"Smile!" and I would answer
"What is there to smile about?"

"Write that down," I urge
us both as we pass the diner
popping with pinball bells,

ajump with light. "What
crazy kind of food could they
be cooking there?" I blurt,

biting my tongue and begging
of the Muse
her forgiveness

(This isn't the time
for fantasy, but *fact*:
the eye alive in the street)

Then unto the barber
—"He's always standing there,"
a girl at the window mutters

jotting down his white suit,
his arms folded in perpetuity,
his monumental bald head

that ushers us toward
the darkened portals
deepening the Funeral Home,

its dripping canopy
like a coffin lid
waiting to clamp shut.

Each glowing clapboard's
a stroke of chalk
on the blackboard of eternity,

so perfectly white
the whole shebang might
rise into heaven tonight!

A turn onto Main Street,
we go feasting
on flashes of imagery:

a stately 1928 engine,
fenders drawn by eagles
pulling strands of firehouse gold,

glides past us. I think
of the gold "5"
Williams watched clanging

through the darkened city,
that his friend Charlie
Demuth painted, gleaming

on a fire truck door.
"Among the rain
and lights," he wrote

—like us, skirting
sunlit puddles, the
fallen sky framed

in odd nooks and crannies
all over town. "Look
down and see

the sky, the clouds.
Look at the mirrors
at your feet!" I shout,

thinking how nice
to snuggle in a hole
the world has made for you,

your job as part of the sky
finally through;
at last allowed to stare

at the home you came from
(all the time intent
on going back).

Yes, everything's looking up.
A fireman's rubber boot
smack in a wavery cloud

as he motions that engine
—hunks of red and gold—
back to its berth, pausing

to smile and let pass
two nyloned women scissoring
long legs over

a slippery patch
of pavement, gliding angelically
while we take notes.

Some big bruiser splashing
his cuff, ticked off,
wipes and smirks.

That dog, still following
with its long pink tongue,
pauses to lap up bits

of cloud, its eyes
mirroring the chills
along the water's spine.

And water itself, crushed
by clumsy shoes,
regains composure,

collecting itself in
the mantra of reflection
for a haiku:

> *Puddles in the street—*
> *at last the dog gets a chance*
> *to see its own face*

We halt for mirrors, too:
a shop of sundry images
browsed by the glare

of the sun cracking through
the clouds that frame us
momentarily, featuring

my own horse face
haloed by the faces
of the kids, and

showing me dawning
to the idea that
this little town

with its one main street
and local shops
is itself a collection

of knickknacks
balanced carefully
on a shelf

in the mind of the boy
who lived where
I grew up!

That is, me—
walking around
a new town,

letting my eye
embrace the real
like a hungry rose

that gulps a drop
of water, like
the roses that

exploded every spring
as my grandmother coaxed
with her clippers and her hose.

All of this pleasure
I squeeze from a morning's rain
in residence around us.

Let me tell my students
that these puddles are fallen stars
they must write down,

whose light will guide them
to where they live on earth,
scattered up and down

the streets we walk
all day, heaven grounded
temporarily, the sky

one constellation shy

Morphology of *Goodbye*

This afternoon I wrote *goodbye*
on the blackboard. I wasn't going anywhere.
But in my self-appointed role
as History of the English Language
a pleasure like none I have experienced
flooded my whole body.
I laughed a bit maniacally
as I crossed out
goodbye's final *e.*

"You see how a word changes, eh?"
I said to the children,
who quietly stared from their desks.
I held up the New York *Times*
and showed the headline that contained
a stark and black G-O-O-D-B-Y.
"The *e* in *goodbye* is going," I pointed out.
You see it spelled the old way less and less.
What once meant 'God be with thee'
has lost some of its history
since I was your age in school."

Unbelievably, the children
did not fall to the floor
dead in horrible positions

THREE FLOWER GARDEN POEMS

1.

Shadow of a bee zigzagging through the grass,
then the apparition of the bee itself, whirling around me
the way, a moment ago, as I uncapped my pen to write,
three crazed sparrows flew above my head, cheeping,
wings awhir, in and out of the garden's iron fence points.
Everything's waking up, 10:17 a.m. The street sweeper
whirls its brushes along the curb, tossing out
more leaves and trash than it sucks in.
What's that big black hearse doing in the middle
of 90th Street, parked like the black shadow
of something terrible hovering in the air, something
we are not permitted to see, though we know it is death
with its awkward black arms thrown open as doors
to hail us in cool October sunlight, beneath the bluest sky.
A lady pushing a baby carriage stares through the fence bars.
"Flowers," she says in a deep voice, as if
she were half asleep. But I long for the shadows.
Shadows and sunlight. Last warm autumn sun
with its hand upon my neck as I write,
stroking me almost, almost saying, "Good boy, Bill,
good boy," because that's what the sun whispers
all summer until the cold comes to make us feel
as if we were *bad, bad,* and raises its strap of wind.
But now the wind is hidden, though I can see the grass
shake in a lower breeze, and on my face and ears
I too now feel the air. The small tree that stands up
so straight and tall in front of me is a good boy, too,
for jostling with the breeze, for stretching toward blue sky
fit so neatly to the edges of the apartment houses,
outlining the other, bigger trees, managing
to hold the sunlight in its skinny arms
a few last moments, like a boy holding his first love

at the beach, when the sun is almost gone
to sleep far away in the sea, the way
summer has nearly left me.

10.18.93

2.

All of us stare at the flag,
as if it were about to do something
between the trees from which it hangs
at the end of the garden
where I and my students have come
to look and write. Suddenly
I remember that I forgot
to take my pills this morning,
too eager to get around the corner
to school, to tell everybody in assembly
about the writing contest they should
enter—and the white stars reminded me
of the pills. But, hey! Here comes
the sun—a little, anyway,
brightening up my notebook page
and not unwelcome in the week that
George Harrison died. December fifth,
and it's supposed to be sixty-five degrees
today. The two guys who seem to have
just put up the flag walk to the far
end of the garden to admire their work.
They seem to stare at the flag in disbelief,
as if waiting for it to do something,
as if the flag were a window that we
could step through into another life
or back into the old one, before it became
necessary to hang flags everywhere, as if
the flag were a palpitating membrane,
a nervous system gridded in stars and stripes,
some membrane of blood and bone and sky
and stars that we must pass through
in transit to another way of thinking
about what makes us whatever we are.
But with no breeze today, the flag is
barely moving. "What would happen if you
let out slack?" one of the guys asks

the other. I sure don't know, so
I keep on writing, as if waiting
for the world to do something—get even
brighter or make the boombox automobile
that I'll compare here to a migraine-on-wheels
disappear as it drives past a block away
in its aura of *boom-boom* and *thud-thud*.
We keep waiting for winter to do something,
too, amidst this run of sixty-five-degree
days, but the winter simply hangs in the sky
like a flag that is neither red nor white
nor blue, or all of these

12.5.01

3.

A woman stares
at me (unkindly,
perhaps) because I'm
badgering my student
to write. He's "thinking
of a topic." He's
"forming a sentence,"
he tells me. I tell him
don't think, *look*—
and record what
you see. Start with
anything, a screaming
baby strollered along
who squawks and stops
when I make a
funny face at him.
I'm good at funny
faces, and why not laugh
again when a flight of
soap bubbles bobbles
by, headed (evidently)
toward the Catholic school
across the street.
If I remember my own
Catholic schooling well
(and why wouldn't I?),
those bubbles might do
those kids a world of good. . . .
"I ate it and I got
sick," one little girl
in a group of school-
kids says to one
of her little friends
as they walk past.
They're holding hands.
The flag put up after

9/11 still hangs at
the end of the garden,
faded, dirty, looped
over itself like a
blanket hung out to
air. It stirs a bit
in a lovely breeze,
though I have sneezed
three times in succession,
to my and my student's dismay.
"Welcome to the wonderful
world of Nature," I announce
to him in my wiseguy way.
Still, I like that red
row of tulips across
from me that stands up
straight in the sun,
showing themselves like
V's for victory today.

5.7.04

NOT ME ANY MORE

I bring in a copy of my first book of poems
because one of my students has discovered it
in the school library, and all of them want
to see the picture of me on the back of it
from the early '70s when I wore my hair very long.
I take out the book and pass it around the room.
The students are aghast. "Where'd the long hair
go?" "You don't look like that any more, Mr. Z!"
"Oh, Mr. Z, this isn't *you!*" they laugh. They're
astounded. They can't believe that the old face
they've seen all year, the face that has yapped
at them, frowned, laughed madly, grown pas-
sionate about Whitman or Williams, that this
worn-out face was once framed by golden hair that
reached to its shoulders. I laugh along with
them. It *is* pretty funny, after all, when the day
comes that you don't look like yourself any more!

TELEVISION

There must be something
I want from this television
that leads me to watch it
for hours on end, hovering
at the rim of its well
where the swirl of colored images
almost slakes my thirst
by expanding into a body
of water stirred by an angel
so immense its coast-to-coast
transmission stops time.
And so it does. And the sofa
falls away from me, and my glass
of soda that I can't stop drinking
in sips so small the desert
on the screen begins to laugh
at us, so beautiful in its every grain
of sand that the wildlife that have
come to die for my entertainment
have no trouble yielding
their little souls to Bambi
and to the fire that consumes
the mother, and the father, and
all the little children who sing
the same song about the detergent
that scours the world whiter
than white

LATE NIGHT

The horror special effects genius
presents the fruits of his labors
to *Late Night* television viewers.
He removes the dropcloth to introduce us
to "Raoul," he calls it, "the thing
behind the window in *Creepshow,* if
you happened to see it?" he notes modestly.

The camera moves in for a tight close-up.
"Oooo, Gawd!" cries David Letterman, as
"Guhhh," the audience responds to this
scaffold of bones over which latex strips
have been baked to simulate rotting flesh.
The genius fluffs up "Raoul's" scraggly wig;
demonstrates how the eyeballs move,
electronically controlled. The mouth can even
be made to smile in a gruesome way.
Another tight shot: the pointy teeth champing.

"Now I am told," says Letterman,
"that this is a *real* skeleton, hmm?"
"That's right," says the genius, adding:
"The crates they come in say 'India' on them."
The audience titters. Letterman, incredulous, asks:
"Gee, I mean, isn't that *illegal* or something . . .
buying a skeleton?" Then he winks
his big blue eye at the camera, chuckling:
"Keep an eye on your loved ones, folks!"
"Maybe that's why the crates say 'India,'"
mumbles the genius, drawing a big nervous laugh.
The camera pans up and down "Raoul's" torso.

"Well, gosh, where do you get these, er,
things?" says the host. "A place called

Carolina Medical Supply," the genius replies.
Letterman pauses a moment, then says: "Well,
I suppose it beats going to Bones 'R' Us. . . ."
Another big laugh. The genius shrugs.
"They have an enormous catalogue—tarantulas,
snakes, rat lungs. . . ." "*Rat lungs?*" Letterman
exclaims, but the genius is eager to share
the tricks of his trade. He shrugs again
as the audience audibly squirms. "Well," he says,
utterly deadpan, "they *do* sell skeletons
made of plastic. . . . I guess they make casts
of the real bones. But the plastic skeletons
are more expensive than the real thing, and
if we baked the latex on the plastic
the whole business would *melt*. . . ." "Er, I see,"
nods Letterman. The genius fingers "Raoul's" ribs
and works the mouth with the controls.
After the commercials they'll be right back
to show us how throats are slashed in Movieland
and how the effect of a bullet fired through the head
can be realistically simulated by exploding
a condom filled with red paint for blood

THE WOMAN WHO DANCED AND TOOK OFF HER CLOTHES, THE WOMAN WHO SANG AND CRIED

"It's time," the MC blurted, "for Danielle!
Direct from Paris and Montreal, the
loveliest of exotic dancers, here
in an exclusive Fairfield County engagement . . ."
and his voice drifted toward the glitter
swirling on the ceiling of the Club Michelle
where I hunched over a piano facing the wall
as the audience summoned Danielle onto the floor.
Next to me, on Fender bass, stood Danny,
and I forget who on saxophone, or the drummer
whose bass drum socked her pelvis into action.
But I remember Danny:
ugly string tie below thick eyeglasses,
forehead shining under greasy wedge of hair.
The lights were down, he could see everything.
Tonight, as leader, he called the shots. No more
crummy houses to paint, no more used-car hustles—
Danny had recently filed for bankruptcy.
I had spotted the notice in the paper.
Of course, I never mentioned it; besides,
Danny seemed untouched by this swipe of fate,
a man who picked himself up, said "Fuck you!"
to the heavens with his hands, and went his way.
Now he was smiling, waiting for the dancer.
He leaned to whisper, "She's good enough to eat!"
with a flash of tongue. I laughed. Always the poet,
I never saw past the literal to the symbolic.
"We open with 'Misty,' real slow," Danny ordered.
"Go to 'Miami Beach' when she drops the veil.
After she does her thing with the chair,
she signals for 'Night Train'—then we take it out."

I nodded. I only wished that I could see her.
This was the first gig that Danny had called me for,
and Danny worked all the time. We had played

together in other groups, but this was different.
It was also my first gig with a stripper.
Every week for as long as I could remember
the show page of the Bridgeport *Post* ran ads
with high-contrast photos of Exotic Dancers:
breasts and hips and piled gold hair. Their lips
stung to a fullness that could sting. The sheer,
the see-through, the halter and G-string mystery.
The No-ones who came to haunt me
when I stumbled on a cache of "men's magazines"
in the back closet where my father hid them,
those bullet-breasted heroines with torn blouses
who fought crazed grizzly bears no doubt driven mad
by the same scent that perfumed the Club Michelle.
And there I was, pulled between fear of Danny
and my craving for a glimpse of flesh.

At eighteen I hadn't memorized the tunes
after three years of working in bands.
I don't know why; but I was good, even if
I had to dive for music sheets and flip
wildly through the pages of the fake book.
Because I could play, Danny had been patient.
Tonight, though, he was boss. "Everything should be
smooth," he told me, gliding his hand through the air.
All night I could feel him glaring down at me
as I made my frantic searches for the tunes.
Blow an intro, fumble for the right key,
and the phone would stop ringing. Club dates were choice—
comics, singers, the women who came in alone
looking for someone to leave with. Maybe Danielle
would take a fancy to me, invite me back
to her dressing room, ask me to drive her home
to a hip Village pad in New York City.
There, after glasses of red wine, she'd select
some jazz sides by her favorite groups, then disapppear
"to slip into something comfortable."
Before I knew it, in she'd leap, to perform
the Dance of the Seven Veils, the one the law
prohibited in Connecticut. Then she'd

swing herself into my arms, gently but
firmly taking me . . . the way it said
experienced women did, in my father's magazines.

"One, two, three, four," Danny counted languidly.
I dug into the chords that led to "Misty,"
craning my neck around to see her appear.
Blue and violet scarves of continual motion
writhed around lean thighs, whipping the huddled crowd
like the colors of wind. Essence of blonde,
on tiptoes, with spectacular breasts
and flaring eyes, big and deep green, Danielle
snaked and darted about the room. My neck
began to throb, but I squeezed my head around
to see her veils dying to the floor, the breath
of everyone, even the women, sighing at her feet.
The drummer hit a Latin beat (the art exhibit was over)
and the audience strained to get what they'd paid to see.
Stuck to my music, I peeked as best I could.
Sometimes my whole life has seemed that way:
nose-first in abstractions, I struggle with
the fly-specks of existence which, yes, do
make their own dainty music, but blow a-
way in the sudden awareness that life's over
there—on the other side of the room!

The Latin interlude was warming up.
Danielle whirled and rhumba'd with a chair
in and out of the corner of my eye.
She caressed its legs and pushed her hungry breasts
against its back. I bore down on the keys,
as if all my skill could rush her to the frenzy
scheduled to close each show at ten and twelve.
Now the chair stood waiting, like a lap,
and Danielle swivelled. Her long legs blazed
in the blue glare for her to stroke at length,
to pet, hands slipping up her thighs until
they met her crotch but then her fingers swam
outward, miming, *No, no—naughty!* and paddled the blue air.
The keyboard capsized in my twisted gaze.

With rimshots cracking on the snare we chugged
into "Night Train" on the wheels of Danielle's
grinding. The drummer stomped on everything,
as if his drums were synchronized to explode
with her hips. She shook, her tassels leaped
skyward, her sex flew at the Milky Way.
Suddenly she turned red in the red eyeballs
of the crowd . . . but why go on? Language is enough
of a striptease. Danielle pranced from the floor.
Danny called a slow tune in the applause.
The scent of sex swirled into mumbled tones
as couples staggered from tables to hug and sway.

Danny's greasy face gleamed like a hard-on.
He smacked the steel strings of his bass guitar
and I remember turning away from his skinny thighs.
I could see them straining the tight cloth of his trousers
as he walked his notes in time to the beat.
He wore his instrument slung low, below
his thin suede belt. I never understood how
that belt held up his pants! And that night, through tune
after tune, I caught his big wrong notes,
like slow-pitch softballs. Without a warning
he pulled my sheets of music away: "You
gotta learn 'em sooner or later!" he snorted,
slamming the fake book closed as my heart jumped.
I knew he was right, but why hadn't *he*
learned the tunes? He worked with the best.
How could he play so badly?

On our break
Danny approached the table leading a young woman
with short jet hair, dressed in a black sequined sheath.
She was tall, large-boned and bosomy, very nervous.
I recognized the milky Irish Catholic skin,
like the flesh of girls I had gone to school with,
translucent as the words of the "Ave Maria." Danny
lightly held her elbow with two fingers
as he introduced her to the band. Sheila
was his "discovery," a voice like an angel, Danny said,

giving her naked arm a pinch as he talked her up.
She would be singing "Moonlight in Vermont"
and would we be so kind as to accompany her?
This courtliness of Danny's was new. Sheila
folded her hands on the table and, when I asked,
told me how she had only sung in Saint Augustine's choir
before tonight, how nervous she was, how she didn't want to fail.
Danny had spent so much time coaching her.
Then he slipped his arm around her waist, smiling
as he raised his drink, but Sheila with her blue eyes
stared ahead, further than she had ever been
from the Sunday morning choir on a Saturday night.

And so she sang, a breath away from me, sometimes
a beat behind, clutching the microphone in her hands
like a prayer book. The kind of voice I'd heard
at church socials, trained for light opera but struggling
to sound like Sarah Vaughan. Emotion flattened to brittle gestures,
the anthology of singer's tricks, the whole corny catalogue
of "I really really mean it." Danny was beaming.
As he wiggled and thwacked his bass I heard him
whispering, "Yeah, baby!" and, "Do it, baby!"
to Sheila, who dangled from a high-note passage, voice
cracking, her skin as white as the snow
in the moonlight she sang about, pale throat,
the telegraph cables, the shadowy blue veins
in her neck, the people who meet in that
ro-man-tic setting, so hyp-no-tized by the lovely
—blowing the lyrics, oo-oo-ooing her way back
to the falling leaves at the top of the chorus,
the sycamore, the Moon. Light. In. Ver. Mont.

Then it was over, the wavering of her voice,
the terror in it. A few palms slapped together
in the darkness and she turned to me, weeping away her mascara,
reaching out with one hand
as she gripped the microphone with the other.
Danny was all over her, giving her *Oh, Honey* and *Baby,*
that was Too Much, and *Sugar, you killed them, they love ya*
as she clung to my arm, blubbering. "You did fine," I said,

"just fine," and patted her hand, trying to soothe her
while Danny slid his hand up and down her back,
moving closer and closer to her ass.
I watched it stroke and pat her up and down,
then one of Danny's brushing fingers popped
a sequin onto my piano keyboard.
For a moment it unfolded in the spotlight,
black as an orchid, burning in the glare
before I swept it away. Sheila broke
and stumbled off the stand. Danny called "Bye,
Bye, Blackbird," and the dancers hit the floor.

I've carried this inside me all these years,
waiting until I could touch it, like the way
I patted her fingers as she cried, only
able to feel, not knowing what to do. Sure
I went home alone. My fantasies of being carried off
on the shoulder of some over-sexed giantess
haven't much come true. I live with them as best I can
in a world where fifteen glossy women offer themselves
in fifteen positions beside the *Times*
and *Voice* as I wait for the downtown train.
I think of how she turned to me that night,
not him, though he was the one she went home with.
I admit, sometimes I've thought I was a chump;
sometimes I feel superior to his need,
to hers, my own. And other times I look at it and say,
"That was it. That happened." Like Danny turning to me
as we bounced through "Bye, Bye, Blackbird," saying,
"Man, wasn't she terrible? I mean, the lowest?"
And he must have seen the disbelief in my face
and read it as awe, as admiration, because
then he said, laughing: "And you know, man,
tonight after the gig I'm going to take
that momma home, and I am going to do her
every way that momma can be done."

For Steve Royal

That wailing chorus by a tenor sax
on the radio: how it brings you back.
Too young for a legal drink, we would sneak
to the alley behind the bandstand at Patty's,
bopping our heads in time, finger-popping the beat
to hear you blow through the back door, anywhere
the management looked the other way
at teenage hipsters sipping expensive cokes,
bent on digging jazz: the Red Galleon
on the Post Road, or the Showboat you played
so often, in Bridgeport our home town.

Your friend my teacher Tony Guzzi
would lean back from the keyboard
and set me straight on local history:
how your name really *was* "Royal,"
what a fantastic pitcher you were as a kid,
but had to stop throwing because of your heart.
You were the biggest name in the workshop band
that rehearsed on Monday nights at Bill's Castle—
factory workers, high school teachers, house painters—
our heroes "The Jazz Giants." And when
you slid from your seat to solo, cool,
your jaw shot out at an angle as you blew
tier upon tier of notes, we all went nuts.

In '62 you went with the Giants to Newport.
All of us shared the thrill; to play (if only
an afternoon set) for the big Jazz Festival crowds.
We young cats followed—Albert, Bob, the three Bills,
one at the wheel with a motel turban towel
wrapped around his head, high on Cutty Sark,
screaming bop riffs as we eyeballed the pretty girls.
When Ted Curson's sax man was hurt in a wreck,

Curson tapped you to fill in. He had ears,
you could make the insane tempos,
spinning out of Getz and Zoot as they flew forth
from the brains and blood of Dexter and Prez,
as even those of us who played no horn
came out of you: those deep saxophone breaths,
the world flooded with air, like being dipped
in pure atmosphere, lungs crying and singing
the truth of what it means to lay the heart bare.
But no, you couldn't stay; your worried wife
cried, the kids waited at home, and the job.
What did we know of that? "Man," we grumbled,
"All Steve wanted was to play." Sikorsky Aircraft
didn't need another tenor man on overtime.

All I wanted then was music, too.
I was coming up, ten years younger than you.
I had my hands on something. One night you called
to offer me a concert at Danbury State.
You even drove me up there in your car!
Al Montecalvo on drums, young Lou Bruno bass,
the best of the new players. We did "Billie's Bounce,"
that Charlie Parker blues, and the "One Note Samba,"
and one of your favorites, "Polka Dots and Moonbeams,"
a dreamy ballad you poured your damaged breath through,
notes twisting out of themselves like the smoke
from your cigarette, the curlicues of subtle figures
caught by how many ears in that college gym?
You seemed pleased with my playing. You called me back
for local gigs, and in the rush or lull of a buffet
we'd slip an up tune by them, "for the band."
How little you said, your movements precise
as your music. Short hair, in dark clothes always,
a cigarette dangling, always so intense.

When your next break came you went with Woody Herman,
whose new big band was ripping up everyone's ears.
How long was it that time, six weeks? A few months

of life lived with all the stops blown out,
then back you went (none of us could see why)
to the factory line and playing high school dances.
At thirty-two, in a clipping my mother sent,
you stared from the Bridgeport *Post*, suddenly dead.
What was to blame—heart, home, job, the popular taste?
By then I'd split to the Apple to go to school. I
turned my back on the one-night stand, the pureness
of going nowhere. I was no fool, I'm still alive.
I sit at the keyboard and play whenever I want.
In the music we loved, I know I will never be great.
I beat my fingernails flat on broken pianos
from fifteen to twenty-five. Finally I couldn't cut
those changes, soured on the drunks and silly ladies
requesting "Anniversary Waltz" that you'd perform
so graciously, stopping to flash the band your weirdo eyebrow
as you mopped the dance floor with waves of Lombardo vibrato.
"Everyone dies of heart failure," my grandmother wrote to say;
a homespun contribution to philosophy
that leaves little room for sentimentality.
Somewhere, on some ex-musician's shelf,
is there one record or tape that preserves
the beauty of your horn? Those flashing clusters
of eighth notes, invisible, lost in the air of an era when
(you used to sigh and say) "All the kids want is that rock and roll."
And jazz was lost again except for the few.
Your beauty went begging—played the cha-cha, played
the "Bunny Hop." What I can record of you, I will:
American music made at night
by a member of the white working class,
bacon and eggs at the Main Line Diner, later.

Richard Manuel Singing "Lonesome Suzie"

I'll stick my neck out
and say it:
I know just how you feel;
just how you must have felt.
The image that poured into us
in the middle of the night,
jotted down on the pad in the dark,
in the morning light doesn't look
like much. . . . The fall
from self-confidence into self-
contempt that I hear in your voice.
Twice I heard you perform,
back in the '60s, '70s. Tonight,
hearing you sing "Lonesome Suzie"
on my stereo, I wonder how
you could destroy your life by hanging
from the throat that made that voice?
I shake my head and think:
How could you *not*?
The beautiful pain of every note
you stretched and pulled, sliding
along the gravel of your man's voice
into the falsetto of the woman within
who is always ready to burst into song
or to shriek. And right now, for a few minutes,
I am carried along by that voice
as I am borne by the twists and loops
of my own penmanship, all the little
nooses from which I've been hanging
for years! All the deathless, useless circles
of ego!
        Now that I've written a page,
I want to stop my own voice, too.
See what I mean? I told you

that I know how you feel,
with your voice crying that way
in the wilderness of the '60s, the '90s,
any time anyone puts the music on
and you sing to the Lonesome Suzie
who must have lived inside you.
That hurt girl part of me, too,
I would hope to touch with song,
but don't know if I can. In this late night,
I make your voice my friend,
as you sing that I should, and follow it—
like something lighted moving into the dark
—into my own sorrow. Not to stand
on some awful chair, in some lost motel,
alone as I am, and fall with a chain
around my neck into blackness, but
to keep on singing as best as I am able,
hanging on to the line, holding on
to your good gone sorrowed voice

LIVE AT THE VILLAGE VANGUARD

For forty years now, ever since
the recordings were released, I have wanted
to track down the people who attended
the afternoon and evening performances
of the Bill Evans Trio at the Village Vanguard
in New York City on Sunday, June 25, 1961.
Sometimes I've thought that instead of
the extraordinary music of pianist Bill Evans,
bassist Scott LaFaro, and drummer Paul Motian,
these live recordings featured the audience
that talked, laughed, jabbered, and clinked
their silverware and glasses throughout.

Maybe some of them know that LaFaro
was killed not two weeks later
in a car accident, leaving behind
on those tracks improvised solos
of staggering beauty on the double bass.
But then everybody knows that these
were "classic" sessions—Evans at one
of his peaks, a trio still unmatched.

Maybe today some of those who were there
put on the CDs (or their scratchy old LPs)
and listen to what they didn't listen to then.
Or maybe they point to their voices
chattering under and around the music,
exclaiming, "Hey, honey—that's *me*!"

One writer claims that he can decipher
some of the dialogue as Evans works his way
through the melody of "Alice in Wonderland":
"I got a new TV—color!" "That brunette
over by the cigarette machine, I think

she has something to say to you. . . ."
"Maris will never top Ruth, but Mantle might."
"The colored bartender waters down the Scotch."
In the introduction to "I Loves You Porgy"
I can hear a guy saying, "Uh, it's something
by Gershwin . . . *Porgy and Bess.*"
Hey, at least they're listening. . . .

What if I could find some of those people
and interview them—*What were you doing
then? Who were you with that night? Why
had you gone to the Village Vanguard? What
did the music of Bill Evans mean to you?* And
there must be some brilliant sound technician
who could "erase" the playing of the musicians
and pull up the table noise and conversation
of the audience. What an interesting recording
that would make—*Live at the Village Vanguard:
The Audience, Accompanied by the Bill Evans Trio.*

They who yelled for waiters, scraped chairs,
one whose cackle ripped across the music
like a dragged phonograph needle, oh,
I've wanted to find those people and, no,
not murder them; no, not smack their
faces. I've wanted to be the one
to sit them down in my living room
and play for them these recordings
made a few feet from where they sat.
I've wanted them to really *hear*
what they coughed through, for which
they offered smatterings of applause.
I've wanted to see them stiffen and cry out,
"Oh, my God! You mean *that, that* was going on
across the room from my martini?"
"I *missed* the whole damn thing
for that worthless man I spent twenty
of the worst years of my life with!"

Too late. Too late for apologies.
Listen. I'm putting on the first track
now. Hear it if you couldn't hear it then,
wherever you are, whoever you were that day

ELEGY

For Bill Evans, 1929-1980

Music your hands are no longer here to make
Still breaks against my ear, still shakes my heart.
Then I feel that I am still before you.
You bend above your shadow on the keys
That tremble at your touch or crystallize,
Water forced to concentrate. In meditation
You close your eyes to see yourself more clearly.

Now you know the source of sound,
The element bone and muscle penetrate
Hoping to bring back beauty.
Hoping to catch what lies beyond our reach,
You hunted with your fingertips.

My life you found, and many other lives
Which traveled through your hands upon their journey.
Note by note we followed in your tracks, like
Hearing the rain, eyes closed to feel more deeply.
We stood before the mountains of your touch.
The sunlight and the shade you carried us
We drank, tasting our bitter lives more sweetly
From the spring of song that never stops its kiss

MY UNCLE AT THE WAKE

On the upstairs porch where later I would sit
on summer evenings trying to write, my pencils
neatly arranged before me on the desk
below the hanging plant that swayed lightly
in the breeze: there you would sit me down
to tell me about life, what life was like.
I can see your earnest, handsome face;
black hair shining in the sunlight, hands
carving the air or doubling into fists
emphatically. You speak passionately
of what lies before me in this world, and
what I most remember of your lectures
is the knife you said the world conceals
behind its back; the stabs it waits to give.
I was so far away from understanding
anything of life, but I sensed *your* distress.

I knew that you had come out of the War,
young, refused to let the Army doctors cut off
your legs when they froze somewhere in Europe,
and lived to thumb your nose and walk away.
The German officer's hat you let me play with
bore a stain on the lining I thought was blood.
In the attic your bayonet hung in its scabbard
from a nail. Alone among cardboard boxes and grandma's
worn-out dresses, I'd push the catch and slide it
out, trying to imagine what had happened.
Dashing, restless, intelligent, jitterbugging
Saturday nights at the Ritz Ballroom, now you
struggled to fit yourself to something whole. Who else
were you telling your troubles to, or were you?
And I was how old—eight? ten? twelve? Or
all of these, and even in my teens, when I first
began to write. You gave me your anthologies

of poetry, my first paperbacks. Their glassine covers
cracked and peeled, but carefully I
mended them with cellophane tape. The *Winston
College Dictionary* that I used through high school
you offered to me—the grail of shining words.

Somebody's collection of quotations
gave me the idea that poetry
was a cinch: just pick out a wise saying,
dress it up in my own experience
and—presto!—I'd have a poem. Except
I *had* no experience to speak of,
nothing that seemed my own, the kind of life
a writer lived. You had wanted to write,
you told me, recounting the story of a teacher
who encouraged you when you wrote brilliantly
about a piece of notebook paper she crumpled
and left on her desk for the class to describe.
In it you saw a crushed world, white fire, the leaves
of a tree unfolding in fog. This was *imagination*, you cried,
digging into the air with your opened hands,
as if you could pull an invisible world out
of the words you spoke. I watched you, straining
to follow your thought beyond the porch where we sat,
waiting for the truth to be delivered. No one
had ever spoken to me this way. My only relative
to get to college, you went on to business school
at Columbia, in New York City. What a school! What a
world you'd discovered, where people really cared
about the mind! (Here you pointed to your head.) You
could sense it in the bricks, on the library steps.
You weren't getting much of *that*, though, in the business
courses—the literature, the high-flown intellectual stuff.
Still, you'd sit in on humanities classes
at the University; the profs never gave you
a hard time, there were so many ex-GIs.

Then you married. A child soon on the way, you
dropped out after a year, never to return.
Is that what you meant when you talked about
the knife? Finally it did catch up with you.
But do you know that because of the light
in your eyes when you spoke of it, I fought
to get to New York, to Columbia, flunking out
of the small college I hated, cutting loose
at last from my mother's apron strings. I wouldn't
be writing this if I hadn't come here, to
New York. And you were the one who sent me.
All of which I put down in a letter
two or three years ago at Christmas when,
on the outs with my father again, I turned to you.

An early memory shows you helping me arrange
tin soldiers atop my toy chest. In stencil letters
it said BILLIE'S TOYS on the door. Weren't we
close by name alone? "Big Bill" and "Little Bill,"
that's how the family told us apart; named
as we were for your father, my grandfather
William. "Grandpa Drunkenshoes," my father
called him, another unpaid Bill in our succession,
who gave his ideas away for a drink
to men who quickly turned them into money;
who could play any instrument with strings;
whose trousers, stained with urine, cloud the picture
I so love, taken at Christmas 1944,
a year before he died. In it, I am helped
to hold the Army portrait of my absent father.
My mother, young and slim, faces me towards
the eye of the camera. My grandmother
smiles as if her husband, nodding in the chair
behind her, wasn't even there. And you
yourself are a star on a window banner,
away at war with all the other young men.

How did my mother, your sister, figure
in the talks you gave me? Did she urge you
to play big brother because my father
was never home, off in his big red truck
fixing broken cars with the secret tools
I was never allowed to touch, my father
lost, lost to me forever, to the postwar
war to make money, now that good times were here?
The truth is, I wanted *you* for my father.
Is that what you saw in my face
when you came to the funeral home? You
called me by my childhood name, but your gray eyes
eluded mine, whirling away
when I questioned you. Why, I wanted to know,
had you sat me down for those talks? At first
you couldn't remember, but I insisted. I recalled
a phrase you used, I think out of Maugham:
"the skin game." That was life, you told me then.
Someone was always trying to skin you alive.
The crumpled ball of paper, the books you gave me—
I made you remember. Your eyes never came to rest
on me. You stared away and said, "Well,
you were such a sensitive little boy, so
easily . . . hurt. I thought if I could toughen
you. . . . You were so sensitive. . . ."

As you spoke I saw my younger self
at our corner window, stunned as my little friends
kicked apart the fort I had pieced together
in my yard with wood from orange crates
that afternoon, smoothing the earth
with my hands, pulling the weeds and pebbles
so each slat would stand. Why was I alone?
What had I done to them, or they to me
to bring such bitterness into my life?
What had they seen in my sensitive face
that marked me? Dusk had fallen, and my rage
mixed with tears as I followed the outlines

of their bodies as they completed their task.
What did you mean by "sensitive"? I should have
asked you that. I should have pushed you for answers,
but it was the wrong time, the wrong place.
What could I have learned that I couldn't guess?
As you spoke I saw my younger self seated
before you. How little I understood!

And I knew then that I would never get
what I needed from you; and at that moment
I forgave you as you excused yourself,
disappearing amidst the handshakes
of relatives you hadn't seen (it was
true) in such a long time. And at that moment
my anger flared anew, burning clean
and away in the useless flame of rage.
And at that moment I knew that only I
could give myself what I had wanted from you.
And with this knowledge cutting at my heart
I expected less of you than of my own father
lying in his coffin across the room

Imaginary Brother

I have had no brother
except the boy in the mirror
who made faces at me,

who made passes at me
when I walked by,
inviting me to the self-love

that preoccupied me
for two-thirds of my life,
until it narrowed my life

to a rectangle of glass
smaller than a pocket
mirror used by any girl,

in which I was the only subject.
Nowadays I close my eyes
when I shave his face,

for really he has no face
at all that matters. Nowadays
he comes and goes. What

have I lost in wishing goodbye
to him? What did he teach me
about myself that had to be

seen and sent away, like
a mirror in a darkened room
that sees nothing until

its face returns to regard
itself, returns to light up
the mirror with its illusion?

UP IN GRANDMA'S ROOM

Saint Anthony is down
on all fours, poking under the bed
in search of the miraculous medal
my grandmother lost.
He'll find it, too. Saint
Teresa watches from her ceiling
corner, breathless that her breasts
have suddenly blossomed roses.
The odor of the incense pyramid burning
in its metal dish follows me
everywhere, rubbing against my legs,
the legs of chairs, like a cat in heat,
the invisible cat my father won't let me get.
From the mahogany box in the corner
Gene Autry yodels "Don't Fence Me In."
There's land, lots of land
where the starry skies are bright
in that little wooden box!
We are happy to let Gene's genial voice
roam around the room, even though
on the other side of the record
he's toting his old .44. A hankie
cut from her vast old silken undies
hangs from my grandmother's waist
by a pin. The thought of blowing my nose
in it gives me funny feelings, like
wearing her underwear over my pants.
But when Grandma strokes my hair
and lifts the hankie in the air, I close
my eyes and honk. Today we are
painting the woodwork of her room
some other-worldly green, slap, slap.
It's like green milk with green bubbles
on my brush. Upstairs here nobody yells

at me that I'm doing it wrong. Maybe
if I am really good my grandmother
will let me look down the front
of her dress again, the way I did
in the living room when I asked her
if I could. After we finish painting
it's time for the magic bottle of ink:
ask a question, tip the bottle,
the answer floats to the bottom
out of the ghostly black . . .
Yes,

    No,

        Perhaps,

             and my favorite:
The answer may not
be given to you at this time.
Sometimes when my grandmother reads
the *Home Medical Encyclopedia*
to see what diseases we might have
or holds the rosary in a way
that makes her mouth and fingers move,
I try to find the panel
behind her closet door
where a secret passage leads up to
the attic, or so I think. (I still dream
some nights of climbing it.) Then
I like to look inside her
books, especially the one where
naked women appear. They all have
flapper hair, penciled eyebrows.
Their breasts are smaller than my grandmother's,
but none of the drawings show me
the secret of Down Below. That
is the secret I want to know!
All they disclose below the waist
are colored pipes and tubes,
like under the sink.
I know from bathing suits that women

do not look like this, Grandma.
Me-ma, I called you in my baby days.
What shall we do today, sweet face
still alive beneath the earth of my childhood?

BASEBALL

We were only farm team,
not "good enough" to
make big Little League
with its classic uniforms,
deep lettered hats.
But our coach said
we *were* just as good,
maybe better,
so we played
the Little League champs
in our stenciled tee shirts
and soft purple caps
when the season was over.

What happened that afternoon
I can't remember—
whether we won or tied.
But in my mind I lean back
to a pop-up hanging
in sunny sky,
stopped,
nailed to the blue,
losing itself in a cloud
over second base
where I stood waiting.

Ray Michaud, who knew
my up-and-down career
as a local player,
my moments of graceful genius,
my unpredictable ineptness,
screamed arrows at me
from the dugout
where he waited to bat:
"He's gonna drop it! He
don't know how to catch,
you watch it drop!"

The ball kept climbing
higher, a black dot,
no rules of gravity, no
brakes, a period searching
for a sentence, and the sentence read:
"You're no good, Bill.
You won't catch this one now;
you know you never will."

I watched myself looking up
and felt my body rust, falling
in pieces to the ground,
a baby trying to stand up,
an ant in the shadow of a house.
I wasn't there—
had never been born,
would stand there forever,
a statue squinting upward,
pointed out, laughed at
for a thousand years
teammates dead, forgotten,
bones of anyone who played baseball
forgotten
baseball forgotten, played no more,
played by robots on electric fields
who never missed
or cried in their own sweat

I'm a lot older now.
The game was over
a million years ago.
All I remember
of that afternoon

when the ball
came down

is that
I caught it

WALKER EVANS IN BRIDGEPORT

> "Evans does not seem to have been in a good mood the day he
> shot his photo-essay on Bridgeport, the centerpiece of which was
> a parade featuring among other things a smug group of women
> riding in a car bearing a banner that read 'America, Love It or
> Leave It.' The women pictured here [*in a different photo*] look as if
> they've already heard all the possible come-on lines any country
> could make. They don't like Evans, and they don't like you,
> either, and if you gave them money they'd take it and spit in your
> eye."—Luc Sante, *Walker Evans*

And yet these are the faces I come from,
with their mouths' edges twisted down in anger
—or in sorrow—like bent machine-shop metal.
Are they cruel or are they beaten, at a loss
when the stranger pointed his camera at them
in 1941, in May or June? One book about Evans
says that he was in Bridgeport then, before Pearl Harbor.
I've looked at all of the published photographs
he shot in my home town: one of them pictures
a black shoeshine boy perched on the boulder
carved with faces of veterans of the Great War
that sits on City Hall lawn. He's waiting for
the parade that will roar down State Street any minute.
(And yes, Evans took that picture of the open car
draped with American flags, though the sign on it
read "Love or Leave America," and likewise he
snapped pictures of squads of marching troops.)
Below the boy's feet, one of which rests on a stone
Army cap, the stone soldiers and lone sailor, popeyed
with wide O mouths, all of their faces the same,
seem as stunned as the three women by what
I imagine is the approach of terror, of death's
chisel that shears away individual features.
Their blank awe expresses none of the anger
that hardens the faces of the women, one
of whom holds a baby who seems to push

away from her. All of their eyes are dark, gone,
as if too much mascara or the holes in their lives
had extracted even the possibility
of vision, however hard they stared at Evans
and stare at us. I admire the fact that they did not
pose for the camera, that they wore their anger
or sorrow like the metal they might have worked
all week in one of the factories gearing us up
for the War. My mother could have stood
in this group portrait, two years away from
my father, three years away from me, soon herself at work
in one defense plant after another, assembling
Thompson submachine guns or the blue Corsair fighter
with its graceful gull wings. These are the
women who fought the war at home, building
the guns and bullets and planes that killed
so many. How should we expect their faces
to look, even with babies in their arms, even
on their day off, at a Bridgeport parade, in 1941?

MY FATHER'S WATCH

In the late summer rage
that strikes me every year, when
I try to throw out everything
useless in my life, getting
ready for school again, I came
upon your watch, a gaudy
Bulova thing with expansion
band and gold trim. You
never wore a watch
that I remember, certainly
not this one. Maybe you
wore it in the War.
I found it in a plastic bag,
like the kind the police use
to keep crime-scene evidence.
The crime scene of your life
where time meant nothing
meant you were free to gamble
your money away and run
around town in your big red
pickup; aptly named, that Dodge.
Nobody ever knew where
you were, least of all time—
until it began to run out
and pinned you to your sickbed,
having its way with you at last,
and you down for the count.
I see your thick wrist now
as I slip the watch on mine.
After a lifetime of doing nothing
more strenuous than moving
a pen across a notebook page,
I have to slide your watch way up
on my arm to make it stay

without jangling like a
bracelet or some souvenir.
I suppose you thought
that I was girlish. You
had names for me that
I won't repeat here.
The watch doesn't work, of
course—it can't be wound.
The stem is only good for
moving the hands around
to no time at all. Maybe it got
in the way of your mechanic's
work, though you could have
slipped it on later. Always later
than sooner, by the time
you came home I'd be asleep.
I might as well have been
this watch you put aside, the watch
that I'll never throw out because
inscribed on the back it says:
To Al—from Jane, Christmas '41.

My Father in the Dream

Taking my arm as he never did in life,
my father leads me through the rooms
of my dream, speaking to me
in a low voice, a voice he never used.
The rooms themselves, unfurnished,
lean from their white walls, listening
as we mutter to each other.

Even as I sleep, I measure
the cost of waking up
to write this dream, the price
this odd sweet conversation
will exact from the coming day,
the day of work, the day in which
I cannot sleep or dream.

Gently, in the darkness,
the life inside us
takes us by the hand,
demanding to be written—
as if no day were coming.
Softly it speaks—
with the voice we always hoped
the night would use
when it spoke to us!

Promising that we would
never be tired again
if we heeded it, if only
we kept on walking
slowly with our dead father,
guided deeper by his hand
into the middle of the room
where we can sit and write
beneath the only lamp

Beetle

1.
So many times
when I was ill
or hopeless
you hopped up
on the bed, to spread
your tail across
my arm, comforting me
with your silky fur.
And as I stroked
you purred until
butterflies of sound
filled the room, the hum
in your throat
lifting me
from my sickness
or depression
as your white tail
rose with each stroke
of my silent hand.
And so I went
on all fours
to sit where you
had made your sick place
in the front closet.
You rested your head
on a rubber boot, purring,
alive despite your misery
as I petted you, telling you
how good you were,
my sweet white cat.
I said your name, the
several names we had
given you over the years

of our lives together:
Bee, Bernard, Bernie,
Beetie, and the one that
finally stuck—Beetle.
(Your real name, Blanco,
had seemed too formal.)
Twelve years since I
had carried you home
that raw spring day
from the Phoenix Book Shop,
where you were born
beside Bob Wilson's
old wood stove, watched
by your pretty mother
and deaf, blue-eyed father.
I carried you in a cardboard
box no bigger than my hands
home to your brother, older
by a year, who sniffed
and hissed. Then, when you
crawled out, all eyes,
he pinned you to the
rug and started licking,
teaching you to clean.

2.
When you took ill,
when you began to retch
up frothy vomit,
puddling the floor,
the young doctor
(after long talks,
sitting patiently
sipping coffee, weary,
seeing that two cats
were the only children
in our house), took
and opened you,

confirming his diagnosis
of the disease
that eats the world.
How could a little cat
(I wanted to know)
have *this,* suffer
this, as my father
had suffered, gnawed
away to yellow flesh
and filmy blue eyes. What
had we fed you, what
monstrosities swam
in the water of your
bowl, in the packaged food
we gave you daily?
For six months we
kept the disease at bay.
I held you as you
struggled mightily,
trying to force
down your throat
the white pill
that would keep you
alive, and for this
you bit me!
Oh, I didn't
want to torture you
any more, I wanted
the gentle young doctor
to come with a needle
to put us all to sleep!
The little hole
you made in my finger
with your fang
mended itself.
Then I had to crush
the pills, which gave you
appetite, and hide

the powder in your food.
Another month or two
and you refused my trick.
I couldn't bear to
chase you with the pill,
you were so thin, the
bones sticking out. Once
so sure of foot, now you
wobbled when you walked,
and for a long time
each step you took
I thought the last.

3.
When I came home
I had to search
the loft to find you.
You were moving higher,
abandoning your haunts
and comfortable crannies.
I'd find you perched
high on a stack
of cardboard boxes
or balanced on the window
ledge, closer to the
sky, the sun, as if
your animal soul
sensed the drift
of life toward what men
have called heaven.
These dislocations
jarred me; in them I
sensed leave-taking,
and of course
I didn't want you to
go, my friend, for you
were my friend, and
though weakened, in your

last months you took
to wanting to be with me
on my desk as I wrote,
something you had never
done, and I was grateful
to lift you up beside me,
for as long as you
would stay. Indeed, I
was so distressed,
in my human way,
over losing you,
that I began to take pictures,
dozens of photographs of
you—atop the bookshelves,
the desk, stretched on
the bedspread in the sun
those times when you regained
your happy self, and could
still play a little, be
kittenish as decrepitude
encroached, rolling on your back,
paws in the air, showing
that the white fur had
grown back on your belly
where the knife had entered.
I clicked and clicked away;
vain photography, that could
keep nothing, finally,
of your gentleness, the warmth
of you against my leg,
beneath my hand.

4.
Near the end
we moved you
to our closet,
a week after you
made your last social

gesture, tottering out
to greet visiting friends.
You had no strength to
climb up on the sofa,
but they helped you,
and there you sat
a while between them,
head swaying slightly,
for the last time
a member of the family.
To the place we made
for you I went.
I lay beside you,
talking, stroking.
No camera now,
no insistent probing
into your final days.
The doctor came
again (you would never
enter the horrible
black carry box
after we forced you in it
to have you "fixed")
and gave you
a medicine he said
would calm you, however
long you had. And so
it did. I had taken
to sleeping lightly.
Every few hours
I rose and crouched
beside you, petting
and talking if
it seemed right,
or lay beside you
if I needed to.
The last night you
woke me. I could

hear the nails of
your paws scraping
against the wall
as you ran, ran in
your sleep from death,
or ran straight to it,
fearless, the way
you charged after balls
of paper that we'd hurl
across the room.
Your legs worked
furiously, though I tried
to calm you with my
touch, with whispered words.
At last the fit
subsided. You breathed
evenly. Phyllis
summoned me back
to bed, but in a few
hours, just before dawn,
I was up again. You
had gone, the body
still, your belly
hair unruffled
by the movement
of breath. I had
my instructions:
to take you to the
animal hospital. We
brought a plastic bag
that Phyllis held, and
when I lifted you
the shock that you weighed
nothing, had become a
mere feather of whiteness
in my hands, staggered me.
Together we wept
and folded you away,

into the carrier box.
I dressed and smoked
and dozed until the hour
came. I put on my dark
glasses and caught the
crosstown bus. A young
woman studied my face,
unshaven, then turned her
eyes down to the silent
box. The intern who
took you looked quickly
into the bag. I caught
a glimpse of your silky
tail, still luxurious,
but couldn't look longer.
I signed some papers and
hailed a cab home. Over
the animal hospital
by the river I watched a puff
of white smoke drift
into the air. Your body,
with its million lovely hairs,
all atoms now, all gone
into a cloud. At the
door your brother paced,
cranky for his food.
I ran the faucet, staring
down into his big green eyes,
thinking how,
in the image
of a small white cat,
death had touched our house.

Failure

I must have gotten it wrong.
The editors of the anthology
didn't like my 9/11 poems. . . .
Maybe I didn't feel enough,
or think enough, or feel
and think enough. Maybe I
am a lousy poet after all,
a failure—just as the buildings
failed, fell. Maybe I am
unequal to the catastrophes
of my time—Kennedy lurching
backwards in the car as he clutched
his throat before the next shot
took off the top of his head. . . .
Oswald crying out in pain on TV,
gripping his stomach as the slug
tore through. And then Martin,
and then Malcolm, falling. . . .
I didn't do much better
for the hundreds of thousands who fell
in Vietnam, on both sides. My poems
from then are best buried
where they lie—in a closet
cardboard box. The bus I'm writing
this on in my notebook has just pulled up
to the Barnes & Noble bookstore across
from Lincoln Center, a place where I
spend a lot of time and money. This poem
won't be in any of the anthologies
on the shelves there this fall.
There's my hopeless face reflected
in the store glass, through the bus window,
falling away from me as the bus
picks up speed heading towards

Ninth Avenue. My old friend Self-Pity
has slumped into the seat beside me.
I can feel him strapping on my bones,
becoming more real by the second,
even realer than I am, more successful,
anyway, in being what he wants to be.
I should travel all the way downtown
and roll around in the dust of Ground Zero
and wail my little complaint there!
I should move among the bereaved families,
confessing my plight, begging them
to listen to my 9/11 poems and tell me
what they think. I should peek
into the thousands of drawers
where the fingers and feet
are kept stored that couldn't be
matched to anyone. Oh, I must have also
failed poetry somehow! What am I
going to do? Give that woman
loaded down with packages
who's just come down the aisle—
get up and give her my seat?

POEM IN FAVOR OF THE WAR

Come, Darkness—
as once, packed in
our wagons with the
tin pans and rifles,
you drifted west
from New England
across the prairies,
later to swoop down
upon the rice paddies
in the gunships. . . .
Cover our faces
with steel again
until we no longer
see what we do.
Lead us into battle
once more, as you have
so often in the past,
with our eyes
blindfolded, our hearts
vested in armor,
our fingers on the triggers
of the world's most
powerful ordnance.
Summon within us
the desire to kill
anything that moves
without our express
consent—male, female,
young, old, pony,
water buffalo, cricket.
Turn our eyes
into gunsights, our
intellects into crosshairs
in which everything

that exists finds itself
a target. Unsheathe us.
Lend us the spirit
of the bayonet, the teeth
of the hand grenade.
Help us to maul and tear
flesh that does not
resemble our own.
And when we have
killed our fill,
allow us to be ripped
apart by high velocity
bullets that leave us
scattered like shell casings
upon the field of dishonor.
Chastise us, cut out
from beneath us the huge legs
on which we so arrogantly
walked into others' lives
whenever we believed
our national interest
demanded it. Shrink
us smaller than
the ego of the ant,
dissolve our blood and breath
in smoke and flame,
crush our temerity
with the weight of our own
colossal legs that fall
upon themselves piece
by piece, in slow
motion, like the
stricken Towers
that no one thought
could fall from heaven

February 2003

MARGE

How to have held you then
and now to have learned
that the tree of your spine
cankered from within

What if I had never
let you go, had kept
my hand upon
your small waist—
Marge, would you
have fallen?

Your eyes of the Meadowlands
bearing before you
the conspicuous breasts
that all New Jersey wanted
to get its crummy hands on
that you would never let me
touch and had to be removed

Then I wanted to hold
more willing waists than yours
against me, then I wanted
trees that opened to my touch
not sweet promises but
the smell of sweet sap
stinging my hands, my lips

Out of sleep I woke
to write this, back
to sleep I now return
again to dream of you
pressed against my hand
in memory where, young

again, I lean my head
against your breasts
to touch my lips where
you still grow upright
from the earth
alive and tall
into eternity

HER PERFUME

After she left—
well, to be more honest,
after I asked her
to leave—she left behind
several bottles of her perfume
(most of which I had bought
for her), by then almost empty,
little heels and slivers
of amber and silver in fancy bottles
I simply couldn't throw out.

She always smelled so good,
taking long, long baths, swishing
fishily in her element
of water, and now and then
I'd come in to watch her as she
lifted a soapy leg into the air
to shave it clean and bright.
Sometimes I caught her shaving
her "pussy"—that's what we
called her—trimming her
like the swards beside an airstrip
where I came in for landings
oh so many times at the end
of oh so many wonderful flights. . . .

How she smoothed on lotions
that made her skin glow
and touched her breast and
behind her ears and under her arms
with the glassy nubs of those
fragrant bottles or puffed a
cloud of spray at herself, out
of which the goddess stepped.

I keep those souvenirs of
her scent on my windowsill
to catch the light, thinking of
how that light caressed her long
red hair, and what the smell
of her did to my head and blood.
I never dare open those bottles
to take a deep breath—that
would be too much. Sometimes
I even think
that I do not want her
back, the odor of her
is so powerful, so
complete, stopped forever
in those glass bottles

POEM

You know what happens
when you say goodnight
and step to the curb. . . .

Just as you begin to raise your arm
to hail a cab, how you throw it
around my neck instead

telling me that before you go
you just want to kiss me a little,
though you know that I don't like it

and you do kiss me, and we do kiss
right there at the curb, and
of course I don't like it

as I taste once again the honey
that floods your mouth
and mine, that seems to need

my lips to trigger its sweetness,
my tongue to run against
the honeycomb lining your mouth

and then I'm dizzy in a way
that drinks can't manage
when the cab comes screeching
like an ambulance

to your side, and still I'm
kissing you, though I don't like it,
for as long as it takes the driver

to wait for you to slither in,
to listen for your address,
and then you're gone, with me
teetering on the curb

as the taxi's taillights
(the color of the lipstick
you've left all over my mouth)
escape down the avenue.

I don't like it one bit
when I hold you like that
and you hold me
and then go away

dropping kisses, those previews
of coming attractions
that I never get to see

kisses fallen to the pavement
like broken pairs of lips
I'm still trying to put together

when I wake up a little crazier
than I used to be, in the gutter
of my bed, already working

like a madman
on this poem

"You Don't Know What Love Is"

For Rebecca Feldman and Brian Roessler

That's what the first line says
of the song I've been playing all summer
at the keyboard—trying to get my hands
around its dark, melancholy chords,
its story line of a melody that twists
up like snakes from melodic minor scales
that I've also been trying to learn, though
I'm no great shakes as a practicer of scales.

Come to think of it, neither am I much
when it comes to love—no great shakes, I mean.
Not that I haven't had my chances.
Twenty years married, I made a lousy husband,
half asleep, selfish, more like a big baby
than a grown man, the poet laureate
of the self-induced coma when it came to
doing anything for anybody but me.
"Now and then he took his thumb
out of his mouth to write an ode to
or a haiku about the thumb he sucked all day."

That's what I imagined my ex-wife said
to our therapist near the end. She *did* say:
"It's all about Bill." She was right.
And suddenly it frightens me, remembering
how, at *our* wedding, our poet friends
read poems of (mostly) utter depression
to salute us. I wondered if their griefs in love
had double-crossed our union, if strange
snakes in the grass of our blissful Eden
had hissed at us, and now I worry,
on *your* wedding day, if I'm not
doing the same damned thing. . . .

I haven't come to spring up and put my curse
on your bliss. Here's what I want to say:
You're young. You *don't* know what love is.
And as the next line of the song goes, you won't
—"Until you know the meaning of the blues."
Darlings, the blues will come (though not
often, I hope) to raise their fiery swords
against your paradise. A little of that
you unwittingly got today, when it rained
and you couldn't be married outside under
the beautiful tree in Nan and Alan's yard.
But paradise doesn't have to be structured
so that we can never reenter it. After
you've kicked each other out of it
once or twice (I'm speaking metaphorically,
of course), teach yourself how to say
a few kind words to each other.
Don't stand there angry, stony.
Each of you let the other know
what you are feeling and thinking

and then it may be possible
to return to each other smiling,
hand in hand. For arm in arm,
you are your best Eden. Remember
the advice the old poet sang to you
on the afternoon of August 4, 2001,
the day you got married.
May you enjoy a good laugh
thinking of him and his silver thumb
now that you've turned the key
into your new life in the beautiful
Massachusetts rain and—hey, now—sun!

WHERE X MARKS THE SPOT

Not long after you had told me, gently,
that you still grieved for your last love,
though that had ended almost a year before,
and that you could have no intimate relationship
with me, maybe not with anyone for a time,
I stopped my fork in the air with whatever hung
on the end of it that I was eating.
My throat wouldn't swallow.
I felt weak and sick, as if it were myself
that I devoured, piece by piece, as you talked away
the hopes that I had put in your lovely face.
It was the old story coming true for me once more,
though you were hardly mine. . . .
When we finished I walked you back to your car;
I don't remember having much to say.
Why would I? Buildings drifted by,
and cars, and faces. Then we arrived at the place
where, afterwards, I would never see you again,
at a parking lot near Times Square.
There I marked the sidewalk with X's
visible only to me: "At this place
I was lost again," they'd say to me
when I walked there in the future.
"Dig here and find what's left of me,
or what I left behind, where X marks the spot."
I felt like the death's-head and crossed bones
that surmount the treasure chest.
I only felt a little like gold coins and jewels.
I have signed the City with these sphinxes
—in parks, in streets, in bedrooms,
in my own apartments. And there we stood,
you and I, hemmed in by the stitches of X's
that could not hold you to me. But X's
mean kisses, I realized, as well as

what is lost: all the kisses I couldn't give you
chalked like symbols on the sidewalk.
After all, you yourself had been marked
by loss, even in your laughter that afternoon
at the show I had taken you to. Bright-eyed
and smiling in the seat beside me, you
stole my glances with your dark, dark eyes
and your long hair. I thought that I had not been
this happy in a long time with a woman
and was ready to become even more happy,
ready to do anything that you wanted
in order to please you, to see that smile come up,
not knowing what you were soon to say to me
as we dined. And when you spoke,
I felt life fall away from me. Again I felt
that I would never be happy. I felt the words
that I had wanted to say to you leaving me, rushing
out of my chest like dead air, until I had no more words
to say. I seemed to cut and swallow my food
as if it were me myself that stuck in pieces
on the end of the fork I had raised to my mouth.
Had I been chewing on my own flesh?
Self-Pity the Devourer took me by the hand
that held the fork, and once again I feasted
on all that was dark and hopeless in myself,
in lieu of all that was beautiful, desirable,
and unattainable in you. And then
I stood beside you in the lot where you
had parked your car, with the X's buzzing
in the air, sticking themselves to you
and me and the blacktop and the cars.
When you reached out to embrace me, I
moved to embrace you in return—and then came
the part that I don't want to remember,
the part I hate: I caught a glimpse of your
face as we put our arms around each other,
and your face said everything to me about
how you had wasted the afternoon, how eager

you were to speed away in your car, a mixture
of disgust and relief that the thing would soon
be over, that I would be crossed out forever
from your life—and everything that I hated
about myself, my stupid chin, my ugly nose,
my hopeless balded head, my stuck-out ears,
my wreck of a heart, crashed over me,
spinning me into the vortex of a palpable self-hate
that I have only ever let myself feel
a little bit at a time, though it is always there

Little Poem

It comforts me
to reach out, half asleep
at three a.m. beneath the covers,
and put my hand on
a mechanical pencil
I thought that I had lost,
as if I should take it up
in my sleep and write
a poem to you who no longer
lie beside me

ANY MORNING

When I do wake up
and feel my body once again
collect itself around me,
I can't help but throw
my arms around myself
in an embrace, happy
for another chance
at the light

Special thanks to friends and supporters Allan Appel, Peter Bakowski, Ellen Bales, Don Bates, Glen Baxter, Star Black, Marilynn Breithart, Renée Chantler, Andrei Codrescu, Marc Copland and Emily Zocchi, Page Delano, Cathleen Dullahan, Janifer Dumas, Bruce Emra, Maggie Ens, Nenette Evans, Mary Federman, Alan Feldman and Nan Hass Feldman, Ross and Gail Firestone, Natalie Gerber, Helena and Zulfikar Ghose, Ian Gonzalez, Jessica Greenbaum, Charles Haseloff, Robert Hershon and Donna Brook, Phillis Ideal, Joanne Joseph, Marc Kaminsky, Paul Kay, Jack Litewka, Phillip Lopate, Bob Nero (1944-2004), Michael O'Brien, Jane and Leo Ouellette, Ron Padgett, Betsy and Philip Prioleau, Chuck Ralston, George Romney, Hugh Seidman and Jayne Holsinger, David Shapiro, Jackie Sheeler, Jared Smith, Alan Sobel, Anna Stoessinger, Janey Tannenbaum, Angelo Verga, Trevor Winkfield, and Phyllis Zavatsky.

I salute the wonderful team at Hanging Loose Press who worked so diligently and brilliantly to make this book: Robert Hershon, Donna Brook, Marie Carter, Dick Lourie, and Mark Pawlak.

Thanks also to my wonderful and supportive friends and colleagues, past and present, at Trinity School, New York City, in particular Jane Mallison, Cindy Muñiz, Tom Sullivan, Andrew McCarron, Margery Mandell, Saul Isaacson, Nancy Elitzer, John Nichols, Michael Gilbert, Sarah Morgan, Brad Anderson, Mary Di Lucia, Keith Kachtick, Patricia Robbins, Joe Scavone, Don Hull, Tim Morehouse, Laurence Lang, and Peter Moriarty. I am also grateful to my former students Sara Doskow, Andrea Goldstein, Sam Marcus, Field Price, and Anna Strasser.

Thanks to the New York State Council on the Arts and to the National Endowment for the Arts for fellowships in poetry that helped me to find the time to write some of these poems.